**• GOLF •**

# • GOLF •

*A round of good cheer*

**Special Edition for PAST TIMES® Oxford, England**

First published in Great Britain by
Constable & Robinson Ltd
3 The Lanchesters
162 Fulham Palace Rd
London W6 9ER

This edition published by arrangement with Punch Ltd.
Copyright © Punch Limited 2000

A CIP catalogue record of this book is available
from the British Library

ISBN 1-84119-197-3

Design and typeset by Tony and Penny Mills
Printed and bound in the EC

**PAST TIMES®**

# • CONTENTS •

'Right. Now let's see 'is ruddy mechanical caddy
find that one for 'im…'

# • ON THE •
# LINKS

## LAYS FROM THE LINKS
### THE HISTORY OF
### A MATCH

Let **A** be the Links where I went down to stay,
And **B** was the man whom I challenged to play
**C** was the Caddie no golfer's without,
**D** was the Driver I used going 'out':
**E** was the Extra loud 'Fore' we both holloa-ed,
**F** was the Foozle which commonly followed:
**G** was the Green which I longed to approach,
**H** was the Hazard which upset the coach:
**I** was B's Ironshot (he's good for a younker),
**J** was his Joy when I pitched in the bunker.
**K** was the Kodak, that mischief-contriver,
**L** was B's Likeness – on smashing his driver:
**M** was the Moment he found out 'twas taken.
**N** was his Niblick around my head shaken.
**O** was the Oil poured on waters so stormy,

try looking closely at
the ball

If you can't putt in
the ordinary way

or looking closely at the hole

or not looking at
either

Again, some do it
this way

or thus

**HOLIDAY PUTTS (PART ONE)**

**P** was the Putt which, next hole, made me dormy.
**Q** was the Quality – crowds came to look on:
**R** the Result they were making their book on:

You might try one
hand

or no hands

Then why not this?

or (being on
holiday) this?

This, again, is excel-
lent in dry weather

We don't recommend
this, but you might
try it

## HOLIDAY PUTTS (PART TWO)

S was the Stymie I managed to lay,
T was Two more, which it forced him to play;
U was the Usual bad work he let fly,

The teetotaler who did a hole in one and offered
cups of tea all round

**HINTS TO GOLFERS**
Mr Punch's patent caddie car

**V** was the Vengeance he took in the bye.
**W** the Whisky that night: I must own
**X** was its quantity – wholly unknown
**Y** were the Yarns which hot whisky combine with,
**Z** was the Zest which we sang *'Auld Lang Syne'*

# SEASIDE GOLF

[1953]

How straight it flew, how long it flew,
It clear'd the rutty track
And soaring, disappeared from view
Beyond the bunker's back –
A glorious, sailing, bounding drive
That made me glad I was alive.

And down the fairway, far along
It glowed a lonely white;
I played an iron sure and strong
And clipp'd it out of sight,
And spite of grassy banks between
I knew I'd find it on the green.

And so I did. It lay content
Two paces from the pin,
A steady putt and then it went
Oh, most securely in.
The very turf rejoiced to see
This quite unprecedented three.

Ah! seaweed smells from sandy caves
And thyme and mint in whiffs,
Incoming tide, Atlantic waves
Slapping the sunny cliffs,
Lark-song and sea-sounds in the air
And splendour, splendour everywhere.

'Did you mark it, boy?'    'Aye!'
'Where is it?'    'On this yer beach!'

*Member* 'That's Brixham over there.'
*Visitor* 'What's his handicap?'

High on the grassy cape I stood,
    Calmly addressed the ball,
And with what power I swung the wood
    For the greatest drive of all
And saw it topple off the tee
And tumble down into the sea.

JOHN BETJEMAN

# · GOLFING ·
# CHIC

from
## GOLF AND GOOD FORM
*By the Expert Wrinkler*
[1904]

IS IT good form to golf? That is a question I have been so repeatedly asked of late by correspondents that I can no longer postpone my answer. Now to begin with, I fear there is no doubt that golf is a little on the down grade – socially. Golf is no longer the monopoly of the best set, and I am told that artisans' Clubs have actually been started in certain districts.

But the real and abiding attraction of golf is that it mercifully gives more opportunities to the dressy man than any other pastime. Football and cricket reduce every one to a dead level in dress, but in golf there is any amount of scope for individuality in costume. Take the case of colour alone. The other day at Finsbury Park station I met a friend on his way home from a day's golfing, and I noticed that he was sporting the colours of no fewer than five different Clubs.

*Old Hand* 'Ah, I heard you'd joined. Been round the links yet?'
*New Hand* 'Oh, yes. Went yesterday.'
*Old Hand* 'What did you go round in?'
*New Hand* 'Oh, my ordinary clothes!'

The effect of the whole was, if I may be allowed the word, spicy in the extreme. Of course it is not everyone who can carry off such a combination, or who can afford to belong to so many first-class Clubs. But my friend is a very handsome man, and has a handicap of *plus* two at Tooting Bec.

**THE NEW TYPE OF LINK MAN**
Tee time

If players dressed the part according to their ability to play—

Things would be different

## KNICKERBOCKERS OR TROUSERS

The burning question which divides golfers into two hostile camps is the choice between knickerbockers and trousers. Personally I favour the latter, but it is only right to explain that ever since I was gaffed in the leg by my friend Viscount — when out cub-sticking with the Cottesmore I have never donned knickers again. To a man with a really well-turned calf and neat ankles I should say, wear knickerbockers whenever you get a chance. The late Lord Septimus Boulger, who had very thick legs, and calves that seemed to begin just above the ankles, used to wear knickerbockers because he said it put his opponent off his play. If I may say so without offence he was a real funny chap, though a careless dresser, and I am told that his father, old Lord Spalding, has never been the same man since his death.

## STOCKINGS AND CALVES

Another advantage of knickerbockers is the scope they afford for the display of stylish stockings. A very good effect is produced by having a little red tuft, which should appear under the roll which surmounts the calf. The roll itself, which should always have a smart pattern, is very useful in conveying the impression that the calf is more fully developed than it really is. I noticed the other day at Hanger Hill that Sir Arlington Ball was playing in a pair of very full knickers, almost of the Dutch cut, and that his stockings – of a plain brown colour – had no roll such as I have described. Then of course Sir Arlington has an exceptionally well-modelled calf, and when in addition a man has £30,000 a year he may be allowed a certain latitude in his dress and his conduct generally.

Try our cork-tipped golf bag—IT FLOATS—and our combination spoon-masher paddle

I saw Lord Dunching the other day at Wimbledon Park in a charming waistcoat. The groundwork was a rich spinach green with discs of Pompeian red, and the buttons were of brass with his monogram in blue and white enamel in the centre. As it was a cold day he wore a mustard-coloured Harris tweed Norfolk jacket and a sealskin cap. Quite a large crowd followed him, and I heard afterwards that he had raised the record for the links to 193.

People engaged in retail trade are not eligible for membership of a certain seaside golf-club. Local butchers have half a mind to discriminate against customers queueing up in plus-fours

15 May 1946

# WHY WE PLAY GOLF

Some people profess to take it up for exercise—

or because of the scenery

or the fresh air.

Others because they like the outfit

or the social side

or the idea that it keeps them young.

But, thank goodness, there are still some who love the game for its own sake!

# • LOSING •
## YOUR
## GRIP

from
### THE PERILS OF GOLF
[1923]

According to a newspaper interview 'a prominent physician,' when asked whether golf could be regarded as a dangerous game, replied, 'The mental stress is perhaps worse than the physical exertion, especially in the case of elderly people who take the game too seriously.'

By some, I've found,
     It's understood
That golf is bound
     To do them good.
Alas! the book
     Is not so plain
They overlook
     The mental strain.

'Sorry I lost my temper with you for calling me a cheating
swine, old man.'

They little think,
    As on they press,
The mind may sink
    Beneath the stress:
But, oh, it does!
    At length, perhaps,
With one big buzz
    Their brains collapse.

'Keep your head still' is the first rule of golf, and Binks means to do so.

*Passer-by, as Colonel Fitzbang comments on the fact of his having got into a bunker, 'Wait a bit Alf—lets 'ear 'im get out.'*

Still, do not grieve,
    For, strange to state,
They don't perceive
    Their fearful fate;
As men possessed
    They carry on;
*They have not guessed
    The mind is gone.*

# A
# · WINNING ·
# STRATEGY

from
## A SUMMARY OF RECENT WORK ON
## GOLFMANSHIP
[1950]

ALWAYS remember that it is in golf that the skilful gamesman can bring his powers to bear most effectively. The constant companionship of golf, the cheery contact, means that *you are practically on top* of your opponent, at his elbow. The novice, therefore, will be particularly susceptible to your gambits.

Remember the basic rules. Remember the possibilities of defeat by tension. Gamesmen are aware of the 'Flurry,' as it is called, in relation to lawn tennis. *It is an essential part of Winning Golf*. The atmosphere, of course, is worked up long before the game begins.

Your opponent is providing the car. You are a little late. You have forgotten something. Started at last, suggest that

'Actually we ought to get rather a move on – otherwise we may miss our place.'

'What place?' says the opponent.

'Oh, well, it's not a bad thing to be on the first tee on time.' Though no time has been fixed Opponent will soon be driving a little fast, a little tensely, and after you have provided one minor misdirection he arrives at the clubhouse taut.

In the locker room one may call directions to an invisible steward or non-existent time-keeper.

'We ought to be off at 10.38.' 'Keep it going for us,' and so forth.

**A LIFT TO THE STATION**
What our Good Samaritans have to put up with.

THE MAN YOU GIVE A GAME TO

OPPONENT. Who's that you're shouting to?

GAMESMAN. Oh, it's only the Committee man for starting times.

Your opponent will be rattled, and be mystified, too, if he comes out to find the course practically empty.

If for some reason it happens to be full you can put into practice Crowded Coursemanship, and suggest, before every other shot Opponent plays, that 'We must not take too long – otherwise we shall have to signal that lunatic Masterman, behind us, to come through. Then we're sunk.'

## MIXED FOURSOMES

In a mixed foursome it is important in the basic foursome play (*i.e.*, winning the admiration of your opponent's female partner) that your own drive should be longer than that of the opposing man, who will, of course, be playing off the same tee as yourself.

Should he possess definite superiority in length you must either (*a*) be 'dead off my drive, for some reason' all day – a difficult position to maintain throughout eighteen holes; (*b*) say 'I'm going to stick to my spoon off the tee,' and drive with a Fortescue's Special Number 3 – an ordinary driver disguised to look like a spoon, and named 'spoon' in large letters on the surface of the head; (*c*) use the Frith-Morteroy counter.

*Woo the opposing girl* is the rule. To an experienced

'Such an amusing man, my dear! He told me yesterday he thinks a high tee is so bourgeois.'

*The Guest (exasperated with waiting)* 'I've a good mind to drive off, but I'm afraid of hitting that idiot in front.'
*The Hostess* 'Hit him where you like dear—it's my husband.'

mixed-man like Du Carte the match is a microcosm of the whole panorama of lovers' advances.

He will start by a series of tiny services, microscopic considerations. The wooden tec picked up, her club admired, the 'Is that chatter bothering you?' The whole thing done with suggestions, just discernible, that her own partner is a little insensitive to these courtlinesses, and that if only *he* were her partner what a match they'd make of it.

Du Carte, meanwhile, would be annoying the opposing

man, by saying that 'Golf is only an excuse for getting out into the country. The average male is shy of talking about his love for birds and flowers. But isn't that ... after all ...'

Du Carte was so loathsome to his male friends at such moments that they became over-anxious to win the match. Whereas the female opponent, on the contrary, was beginning to feel that golf was not perhaps so important as sympathetic understanding.

By the twelfth hole Du Carte was able to suggest, across the distance of the putting green, that he was fast falling in love. And by the crucial sixteenth Female Opponent would have been made to feel not only that Du Carte had offered a proposal of marriage but that she, shyly and regretfully, had refused him.

Du Carte invariably won these matches two and one. For he knew the First Law of Mixed Gamesmanship: that *No woman can refuse a man's offer of marriage and beat him in match play at the same time.*

STEPHEN POTTER

THE PERFECT LOSER

# THE
# • CADDIE •

from
GOLFING RHYMES

## YOU AND
## YOUR CADDIE
[1925]

IN private life you may be choicely good,
Deserve high praise as uncle or as daddy,
You may, in fact, be everything you should,
But no man is a hero to his caddie.

You may have pictures, priceless curios,
A famous fiddle (half of it spells stradi);
You've taken prizes with a home-grown rose,
But you are not a hero to your caddie.

You've headed expeditions to the Pole,
    Encountered dervishes near Halfa (Wady);
You've set your teeth and done without the dole,
    But you are not a hero to your caddie.

You've written deathless prose and cunning rhyme,
Composed a song, a second *Yip-i-addy*;
You deal yourself four aces every time,
    But you are not a hero to your caddie.

*Chastened Diehard* 'Might I trouble you for the
niblick, comrade?'

*Sensitive Golfer (who has foozled)* 'Did you laugh at me, boy?'
*Caddie* 'No, Sir; I was laughin' at anither man.'
*Sensitive Golfer* 'And what's funny about him?'
*Caddie* 'He plays gowf awfu' like you, Sir!'

And yet it is not difficult to be
A source of satisfaction to the laddie
*Largesse oblige* – in terms of £ s.d.
You may become a hero to your caddie.

*Jaded Golfer to negligent caddie* 'Take a little more interest in your work my lad. It may be irksome, but remember you can't hate this game more than I do.'

from
# GOLFERS AS I 'AVE KNOWN
## [1906]

GOLFERS I divides in me own mind into three clarses; them as 'its the ball, them as skratches it, and them as neither 'its nor skratches the blooming ball but turns rarnd and wants to 'it or skratch anyone as is small and 'andy. The first clars is very rare, the second is dreadfull plentifull, and the third, thank 'evins, can jeneraly be kep clear of by them as knows the ropes. Sich as meself.

Any himprovement in golfers, as a clars, is doo to the

*Caddie (as the last club goes west)* 'That's done it! Now you've only got yer umbreller.'

'uge morril hinfluence of us caddies, 'oom some pretends to look down on. Much can be done, even wif the most 'ardened (and some of them golfers is dreadfull 'ardened), by firmness and hexample. 'Show 'em from the fust as you'll stand no nonsense,' is allus my words when the yunger caddies gathers ararnd me fer hadvice. Me being older than me years, as the sying is, and much looked up to. If, as I often 'ears say, there's less of langwidge and more of golf upon these 'ere links, it's doo in no small part to 'im 'oo pens these lines. 'Oo's 'onnered nime is 'ENERY WILKS.

A SUGGESTION

Ear blinkers for caddies of tender age in attendance on hot-tempered Anglo-Indian military gentlemen learning golf.

41

# THE
# • PRO •

from
## A ROUND WITH THE PRO
[1929]

If any perfection
    Exists on this earth
Immune from correction,
    Unmeet for our mirth,

The despair of the scoffer,
    The doom of the wit,
A professional golfer,
    I fancy, is it.

No faults and no vices
    Are found in this man,
He pulls not nor slices,
    It don't seem he can;

# THE HOLIDAY SWING

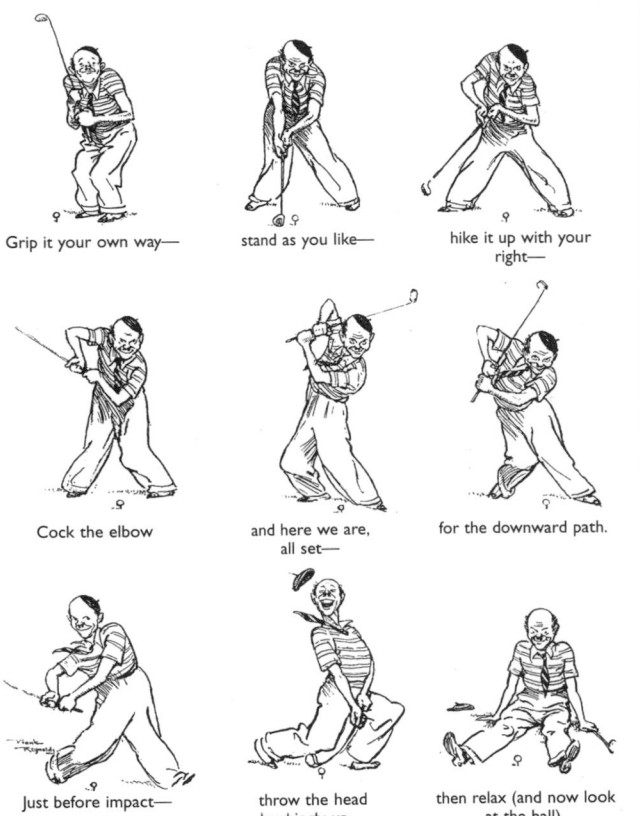

Grip it your own way—

stand as you like—

hike it up with your right—

Cock the elbow

and here we are, all set—

for the downward path.

Just before impact—

throw the head laughingly up—

then relax (and now look at the ball).

Like an angel from heaven,
  With grief, not with blame,
He points out the seven
  Worst faults in your game.

'You should hold your club *this* way,'
  He tells you, 'not *that.*'
You hold your club his way
  It hurts you, my hat!

You mark his beginning,
  You watch how be ends,
You observe the ball spinning,
  How high it ascends!

You copy his motions,
  You take it like *this*,
You seize all his notions
  You strike – and you miss.

You aim with persistence,
  With verve and with flair,
You gaze at the distance
  The orb is not there.

The hands have been lifted,
  The head remains still,
Your eyes have not shifted
  No, nor has the pill.

45

He points out the errors
    He told you before,
To add to your terrors
    He points out two more,

And the ball goes careering
    Far into the sky
And is seen disappearing
    Due south, over Rye.

You stand staring wildly
    (It's now at Madrid)
And the pro. remarks mildly,
    'You see what you did?

You made every movement
    I've tried to explain;
That shows great
    improvement,
        Now do it again.'

                    EVOE

*Professional Golfer (in answer to anxious question)* 'Weel, no Sir, at your time of life, ye can never hope to become a *player*, but if you practise hard for three years, ye may be able to tell good play from bad when ye see it!'

There's a lot more in golf than just hitting a little ball', says a professional. There's missing it for instance.

*3 August 1938*

*First Enthusiast* 'I say, will you play another round with me on Thursday?'
*Second Enthusiast* 'Well, I'm booked to be married on that day—*but it can be postponed!*'

# • MARTYRS •
# TO THE
# COURSE

from
## THE GOLF WIDOWS
[1902]
*(After E. B. Browning)*

Do you hear the widows weeping, O my brothers,
    Wedded but a few brief years?
They are writing home complaining to their mothers,
    And their ink's suffused with tears.
The young lads are playing in the meadows,
    The young babes are sleeping in the nest;
The young men are flirting in the shadows,
    The young maids are helping them, with zest.
But the young golf widows, O my brothers,
    They are weeping bitterly,
They are weeping in the playtime of the others,
    While you're swiping from the tee.

**THE GOLF MANIAC PROPOSES**

Do you ask your grazing widows in their sorrow
    Why their tears are falling so?
'Oh – yesterday – to-day again – tomorrow –
    To the links you ALWAYS go!
Your golf "shop,"' they say, 'is very dreary,
    You speak of nothing else from week to week;
A really patient wife will grow a-weary
    Of talk about a concentrated cleek."
Yes, the young golf-widows, O my brothers,
    Do you ask them why they weep?
They are longing to be back beside their mothers,
    While you're playing in a sweep.

*Bride (determined to share her husband's troubles)* 'Dearest, go on
telling me about the worm-casts on the seventeenth.'

'I want some golf-balls for a gentleman, please.'
'Certainly, Madam. What sort does he like?'
'Well, the only time I ever saw him play he used a small white ball.
But I cannot say I gathered the opinion that he exactly liked it.'

'I'm glad my husband's bought a billiard-table; it takes
his mind off golf.'


And well may the widows weep before you
    When your nightly round is done;
They care nothing for a stymie, or the glory
    Gained by holing out in one.
'How long,' they say, 'how long in careless fashion,
    Will you stand, to drive the Dyke, upon our hearts,
Trample down with nailèd heel our early passion,
    Turning homeward only when the light departs?
You can hear our lamentations many a mile hence,
    Can you hearken without shame,
When our mourning curseth deeper in the silence
    Than a strong man off his game" ?

# THE · CLUBHOUSE ·

## THE OLDEST MEMBER

[1925]

OUR oldest Member, I may say,
Will soon be gently put away;
He makes the Secretary's life
An endless round of storm and strife;
He badgers members of Committee
With fool complaints about the 'pretty;'
He goes and buttonholes the Pro,
And asks him if he doesn't know
There is a worm-cast on the seventh
And heaps of mole-hills block the eleventh,
And why the sand in tee-box nine
Is so exceptionally fine.
The Oldest Member is a bore;
He does not set us in a roar
With memories of bygone years –

No, he reduces us to tears.
His stories of the past repel;
He does not even tell them well.
In ev'ry way the man's a curse,
And I'm afraid *he's getting worse*.

'Ay, and let me tell you, Sir, I was playing golf before
your were bor-r-rn!
'Played much since?'

# THE ESSENTIALS OF GOLF.

## [1920]

'Do you know anything about golf?' I asked Pottlebury by way of making conversation with a comparative stranger, and immediately afterwards knew I had made a mistake. I should have inquired 'Do you golf?' or 'Are you a golfer?' and no evasion would have been possible.

'I should think I do,' he replied 'I suppose there's hardly a course between here and Strathpeffer that I haven't visited. English and Scottish I know them all.'

'And which is your favourite course?'

'That is a difficult question,' he remarked judicially. 'Only last night I was arguing about the comparative merits of Westward Ho! and St Andrews. Both are easily accessible from the railway, but if you take your car the latter is to be preferred. You get your life bumped out of you on those North Devon roads.'

'I wasn't thinking of the travelling facilities,' I observed coldly.

'No, of course. It's what you find at the other end that counts. Well then, travelling aside, there is much to be said for Sandwich. The members' quarters are comfortable –very comfortable.'

I must have made a disparaging gesture, for he immediately continued

'But if it's only lunch you want, I advise those

Lancashire clubs round Southport. They know how to lunch in those parts – Tweed salmon, Welsh mutton and Whitstable oysters.'

'No doubt your judgment is correct,' I replied, 'but I –'

'And at one of them they keep a real French *chef* who knows his business. I wouldn't wish for a better cuisine anywhere.'

'There are other things,' I remarked loftily, 'besides those you mention.'

'Exactly; that's why I like to see a good bridge-room

*Proud Member* 'Now, tell me, how did you find our greens?'
*Distinguished Visitor* 'Well, you **see**, they had flags on them!'

AFTER LUNCH
'We've got this for a possible half, Partner—rather a
forgone hope, eh?'
'My dear chap, aren't you thinking of a forlorn conclusion?'

attached and enough tables to accommodate all comers. They have that at Spotworth. You can often get a game of poker as well.'

'But don't you see,' I exclaimed, 'that all these things are mere accessories and circumstances?'

'That is true,' he murmured; 'they are but frames as it were of the human interest. After all there's nothin to equal a crowd of jolly good fellows in the smoking room. I've had some excellent times down at Bambury – stayed yarning away to all hours. Some of the best fellows I ever met belonged to that Club.'

'You don't talk at all like a golfer,' said I.

Pottlebury laughed. 'I was forgetting. If it's whisky you want you can't beat Dornoch and Islay. We've nothing in England to touch them. Why, I've met some of the

'No, thanks—I'm driving!'

keenest golfers of the day at Islay – nothing less than a bottle a day apiece.'

'Sir,' said I severely, 'it is clear that you have never struggled like grim death with an opponent who was three up at the turn until you were all square at the seventeenth, and then found yourself after a straight drive with an easy baffy shot to –'

'One moment,' said Pottlebury; 'what exactly *is* a baffy?'

## THE STEWARD

Presiding at the bar.
This man is popular:
He hears a lot of tommy-rot.
Like 'Did the eighth in par.'

He never says 'Oh fie!'
Or. 'What a beastly lie!'
He simply grins
And mixes gins
And puts a little by.

*23 September 1925*

from
# LETTERS TO THE SECRETARY
## OF A GOLF CLUB
[1934]

*From General Sir Armstrong Forcursue, K.B.E., C.S.I.,*
*'The Cedars', Roughover.*
*Monday, 14th May, 1934*

SIR,—What in the name of fortune do those bounders on the Committee mean by raising my handicap from 22 to 24? If, as I scarcely credit, they are under the impression I cannot play to 22 I would have them know that I won the Cadaverabad Monthly Medal in February, 1908, and the Ladies' Autumn Vase at Putridshindi in 1920. What's more, on both these occasion I played off 21.

Your immediate explanation of this piece of impertinence is anxiously awaited, and I warn you, Sir, that if the Committee do not take prompt action and arrange that my handicap be again fixed at 22 I shall resign from the Club.

> Yours faithfully,
> ARMSTRONG FORCURSUE

*From Lionel Nutmeg, Malayan Civil Service, Retd.,*
*Old Bucks Cottage, Roughover.*
*14th May*

DEAR MR. SECRETARY,—Kindly convey my sincere con-

Ex-Private Smith finds there is still considerable use for certain portions of his field equipment whilst carrying for the General.

gratulations to the Committee for putting up General Forcursue's handicap from 22 to 24.

The information with which I reluctantly felt compelled to supply them was in no way exaggerated, for, playing with him as I do at least once a week, I flatter myself that no one could be in a better position to pronounce a fairer or a more just statement as to his golfing capabilities.

     Yours sincerely,
     L. NUTMEG.

PS. Perhaps this would be an opportune moment to suggest that my own handicap be now lowered from 23 to 22. I did the 8th in '3' on Saturday.

*From Dr. Edwin Socket, Roughover.*
*(By messenger)*
*Monday, 14/5/34.*

DEAR WHELK,—For Heaven's sake have the General's handicap put back to 22. Since the Committee raised it to 24 his blood-pressure has gone up from 170 to well over 200, and when I saw him last, not half-an-hour ago, it showed no signs of easing.

Lady Madge says she finds it quite impossible to sit in the same room with him, and from what I hear you must be going through hell at the Club.

Sincerely yours,
E. SOCKET

'You play your shot, Colonel. I'll finish the story after.'

DEAR MR. SECRETARY,

I am in receipt of your letter of Saturday the 19th, from which I note that the Committee have now put back my handicap from 24 to 22.

While thanking you for your attention to this matter, I should like to point out that it is of no real moment to me what figure I play off, for, as you are aware, I always make a point of never taking my golf seriously.

Yours very sincerely,
ARMSTRONG FORCURSUE

'That's a better one, Sir. You got a—a bit o' somethin'
over that time, Sir.'

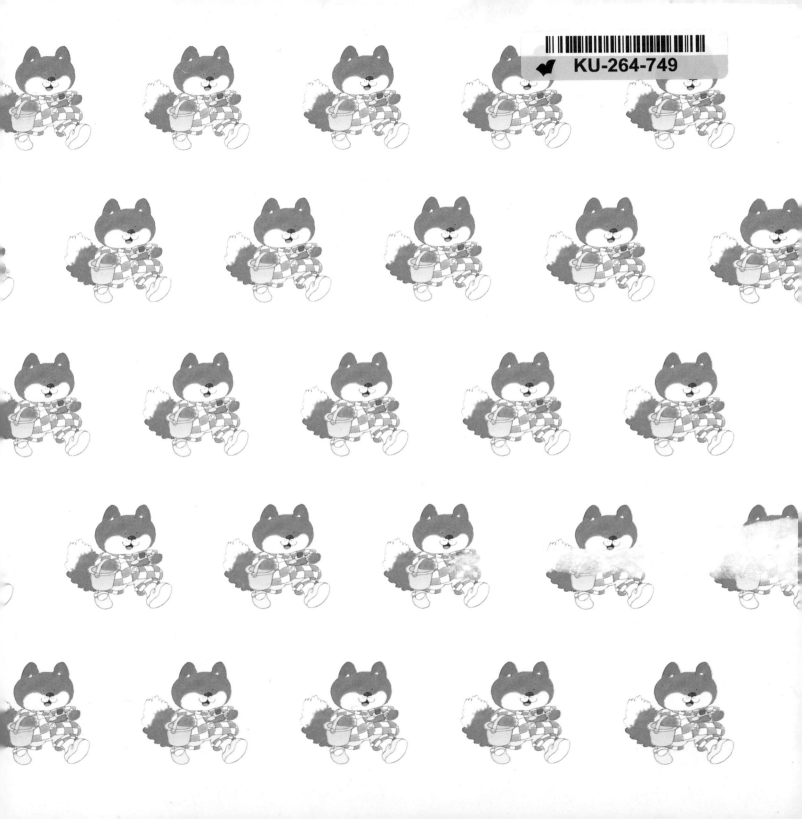

First published in hardback in Great Britain by HarperCollins Publishers Ltd in 1997

1 3 5 7 9 10 8 6 4 2
ISBN 0 00 198219 2 (HB)

First published in Picture Lions in 1997
1 3 5 7 9 10 8 6 4 2
ISBN 0 00 664564 X (PB)

Picture Lions is an imprint of the Children's Division, part of HarperCollins Publishers Ltd.
Text and illustrations copyright © Colin and Jacqui Hawkins 1997
The author/illustrators assert the moral right to be identified as the author/illustrators
of the work.
A CIP catalogue record for this title is available from the British Library.

Printed and bound in Hong Kong.

# FOXY

## and his Naughty Little Sister

## Colin and Jacqui Hawkins

Collins

*An Imprint of HarperCollinsPublishers*

Sometimes Foxy's little sister was naughty, but she didn't mean to be. One day she was playing in the bathroom.

Splish! Splash! Splosh!

There was water everywhere.

"What a mess!" grumbled Foxy,
as he squelched across the floor.
"I'm sorry," said his little sister.
"It was an accident."
It took a long time to mop up.

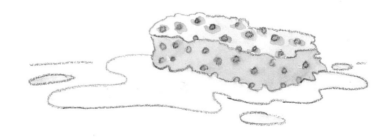

The next day Foxy's little sister played with his kite without asking.

"Whee! This is fun," she laughed, as the kite swooped around the sky.

# WHOOSH!

The wind blew the kite high into a
tree where it got tangled up.
"Oh no! Look what you've done!"
cried Foxy.
His kite was torn and broken.
"I'm sorry," said his little sister.
"I didn't mean to do it."

Later that day Foxy could not find
Teddy. He searched everywhere.

"Have you been playing with Teddy?"
Foxy asked his little sister.
"Oh!" she cried. "I think I left him
in the garden."

Quickly Foxy ran to the back door.
There huddled in a soggy heap was
poor Teddy. It was raining and Teddy
was very cold and very wet.

"Look at Teddy," shouted Foxy.
"You're so naughty!"
"I'm sorry," mumbled his little sister.
Poor Teddy!

The next day Foxy's little sister invited
her best friend to play.
Her best friend was
*really* naughty.

She jumped up and down on the sofa.

BOING!

TWANG!

And she hit Foxy
with a cushion.

BIFF!

She spilt her drink and threw her food.

# SPLAT!

She kicked a football through the window.

# SMASH!

She broke Foxy's favourite toys.

SNAP!

CRACK!

She scribbled all over the walls.

# SCRAWL!

She tore
Foxy's
comics.

# RIP!

And she stuffed toilet rolls down the toilet.

# PLOP!

She threw Teddy down the stairs.

BUMP!
THUMP!

She lifted up her dress and showed her knickers. Then she screamed at the top of her voice.

WHAAAH!

And she never once said sorry.

Foxy and his little sister were so
glad when she went home.
"She's not my best friend any more,"
said Foxy's little sister.
"She's the naughtiest person
I know!"

Foxy grinned at his little sister.
"Perhaps you're not so naughty
after all," he said.

And he meant it.

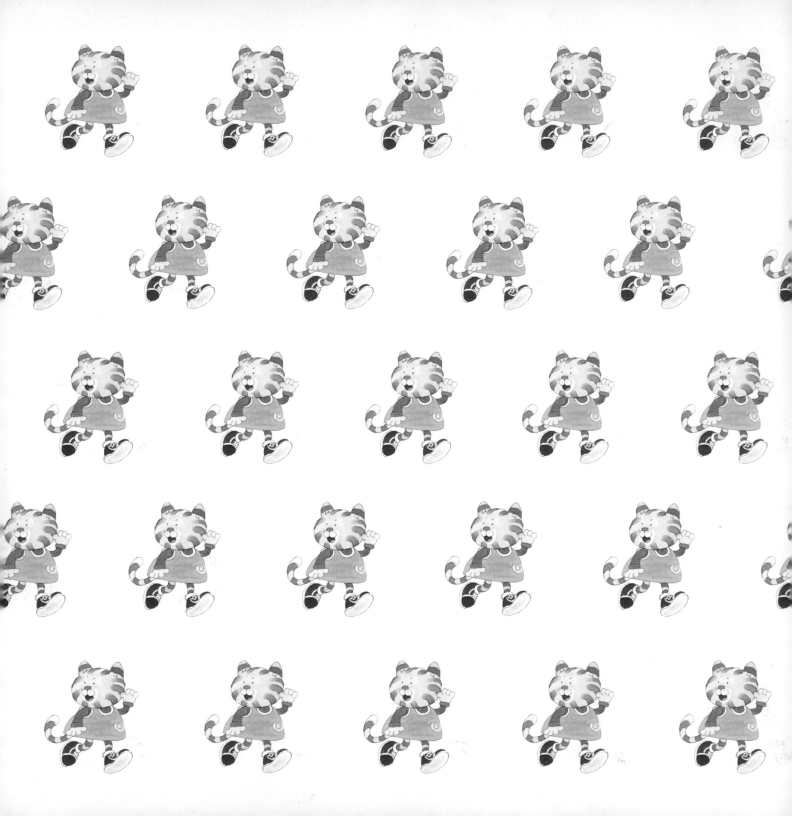